String EXPLORER
A Journey into the Wonders of String Playing

Andrew Dabczynski • Richard Meyer • Bob Phillips

VIOLIN
Book 2

Welcome back, String Explorers!

Your adventure of a lifetime continues as we begin Book 2! Together, we will explore even more wonderful music from the past and present, and melodies from around the world. We've already set sail aboard our noble schooner MUSICIANSHIP, so get ready to encounter many new exciting challenges as we journey across the vast Sea of Knowledge to reach our goal: the Lands of Golden Harmony!

The Explorer's Map on page 48 will help you keep track of your progress. Grab your instrument and come along!

Good luck, Explorers!

The authors would like to thank Kim Kasabian, Pam Phillips, Greg Plumblee and Kate Westin for their help with the editorial development and production of this series.

Illustrations: John Kachik
Instrument Photos: Steve Kuzma Photography

ISBN 0-7390-3070-1

Arco Dakota

Rosalyn Le Bow

THE ADVENTURE CONTINUES...

Exploring Tuning

The tuning peg for each string is labeled in picture A. Turning the peg **away** from you tightens the string, making the pitch **higher**. Turning the peg **towards** you loosens the string, making the pitch **lower**. We will explore four different ways to tune.

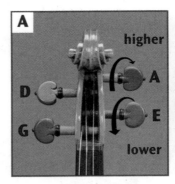

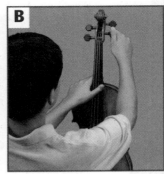

Tuning Pizzicato

1. Violin in Your Lap (pictures B and C)

With the violin in your lap, put your thumb and first finger around the peg of the string you are tuning. Turn the E and A pegs with your right hand (B), and turn the G and D pegs with your left hand (C). With your other hand, pluck the string.

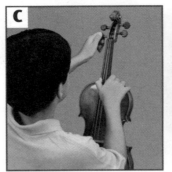

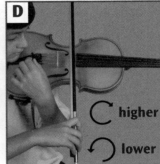

Tuning with the Bow

2. Using the Fine Tuner (picture D)

In playing position, put your left thumb and first finger around the fine tuner of the string you are tuning, and play the string with your bow. Turning the fine tuner to the **right** tightens the string and makes the pitch **higher**. Turning the fine tuner to the **left** loosens the string and makes the pitch **lower**. Remember: **Righty Tighty, Lefty Loosey**. All of your strings probably have fine tuners.

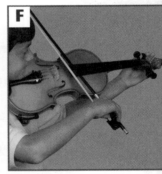

3. Violin on Your Knee (picture E)

With the violin scroll supported by your knee, use your left thumb and first finger to turn the peg of the string you are tuning. Play the string with your bow.

4. Using the Tuning Pegs in Playing Position (pictures F and G)

Use your left thumb and first finger to turn the peg of the string you are tuning as you play the string with your bow.

Echo Tuning Activities

Activity 1

Watch and listen as your teacher echoes the tuning note on the CD recording and demonstrates tuning the A string.

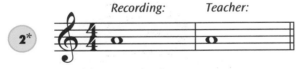

*Numbering corresponds to track numbers on the String Explorer CD.

Activity 2

Sing the tuning note A.

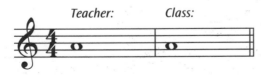

Activity 3

Listen as your teacher plucks the tuning note A four times. With your violin positioned in your lap as in the instructions for tuning method 1 above, pluck the tuning note A four times. Does your note sound the same as your teacher's or is it too high or too low? Tune your string as necessary so that it matches your teacher's.

Activity 4

Listen as your teacher plays the tuning note A four times. Using either tuning method 2, 3, or 4 above, bow the tuning note A four times. Is your note the same as your teacher's, or is it too high or too low? Tune your string as necessary.

Activity 5

Echo the tuning note. Is yours the same or is it too high or too low? Tune your string as necessary.

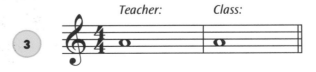

Activity 6

Now tune all of your strings using track 3 of the *String Explorer Accompaniment CD*. First tune the D string, then the G string, and finally the E string.

Exploring Vibrato

Now it's time to learn vibrato—a steady, gentle rocking of the hand. This action, which has been used by string players for centuries, will make your playing sound more expressive.

Activity 1: High Fives

1. Holding the violin in banjo position, place the "fat" part of your thumb on the round, curved end of the neck where it meets the violin body. Extend your fingers, like you're giving a "high five" (A).

2. Now, steadily and gently pat your palm against the shoulder of the violin, like you're giving a gentle high five (B). Keep a steady beat. Try patting the rhythms "motorcycle, stop, stop," or "run pony, run pony." Or, try patting the rhythm of your name (for example, "Ar-co Da-ko-ta").

3. Practice steps 1 and 2 with your violin in regular playing position.

Activity 2: Wire Gliders

1. Holding the violin in banjo position, do the same "high five" motions again (A and B). Then, do the same thing in playing position, allowing your second finger to gently touch the A string (C).

2. Let your second finger glide up and down the string while you pat the shoulder of the violin with your palm (D). Now you're doing "Wire Gliders!" Try practicing using the same rhythms as for "High Fives." Next, try "Wire Gliders" using your third finger, then your fourth, and finally your first finger. Practice using each finger on each of the four strings.

A string

Activity 3: Rubber Band Twangs

1. With the violin in playing position, slide your hand up the neck until the "fat" part of your thumb rests on the round, curved end of the neck where it meets the violin body. Let your palm rest against the shoulder of the instrument.

A string

2. Place your second finger securely in 3rd position on the A string, fingering the note E (be sure to pick up your first finger and hold down only the second finger). Roll your finger slightly away from you (E), as if you're pulling back on a tightened rubber band. Then, let your finger rebound back to its original position, as if the rubber band was "twanging" it forward (F). Now try two "twangs" in a row, keeping a steady beat.

3. Practice this exercise while playing with the bow. Slur two, then three, then four twangs in one bow, always keeping a steady beat. Try to gradually increase the speed of the twanging motion, perhaps using a metronome to keep your beat steady.

E string

4. Now practice "Rubber Band Twangs" using your second finger in 3rd position on each of the other strings. Next, practice using your third, then fourth, then first finger on the A string, and then on each of the other strings (be sure to hold down only one finger at a time). Finally, try "Rubber Band Twangs" with each finger on all four strings, this time in 1st position.

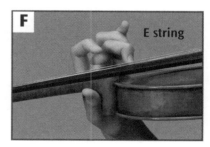

E string

Activity 4: Dies Irae

Play the following exercise to practice your vibrato.

Dies Irae

III (This exercise may also be played in 3rd position after completing Unit 4.)

UNIT 1

Ready, Set, Bow

**Right Hand Review,
Détaché, Marcato**

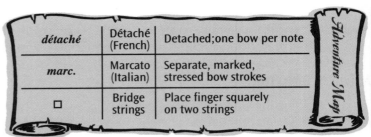

détaché	Détaché (French)	Detached; one bow per note
marc.	Marcato (Italian)	Separate, marked, stressed bow strokes
□	Bridge strings	Place finger squarely on two strings

Adventure Map

Detached in D (review of quarter notes, quarter rests, eighth notes)

Practice: 1. Clap & count 2. Arco using détaché bowing

Half and Half (half notes, half rests)

Arches and Tunnels (slurs, hooks)

Waltzing Ties (¾ meter, dotted half notes, ties)

Pick Up a Quarter (pickup notes, dotted quarter notes)

Machu Picchu Stomp (whole notes, double stops, fermata)

Hidin' a Surprise (²⁄₄ meter, accents, eighth rests)

Play all eighth notes marcato.

Syncopated Two-Step (syncopation, tenuto) (Every time you see a word in this color box, look it up on page 47.)

4

Finger Tips

Key Signature Review, Bridging Strings with One Finger

D Major Scale (solfège)

13

Sing: Do Re Mi Fa Sol La Ti Do...

D Major Arpeggios

14

G Major Scale

15

G Major Thirds

16

C Major Scale

17

C Major Thirds

18

F Major Scale

19

F Major Arpeggios

20

Now play lines 13–20 with the following bowings:

a.   b.   c.   d.   e.   f.   *marc.*

Now play lines 13–20 with the following rhythms on each note:

a.   b.   c.   d.   e.   f.

5

Putting It Together

6

This Is the Place

Traditional American Folk Song

The Happy Farmer

Robert Schumann (1810–1856)

ARCO'S HISTORY HIGHLIGHTS

Many famous composers wrote music that was originally intended to be performed as part of a play. Such special music, which is meant to be played before, after, or between acts of a play, is called *incidental music*. This well-know **nocturne** is part of the music Felix Mendelssohn composed for Shakespeare's play *A Midsummer Night's Dream*. Do you think background music used in television and movies is the same as incidental music? Why or why not?

Nocturne (Duet)
from A Midsummer Night's Dream

Felix Mendelssohn (1809–1847)

Ready, Set, Bow

Sixteenth Notes, Fortissimo, Pianissimo

♫♫	Sixteenth notes	One-quarter beat each	♫♫ = ♩
ff	Fortissimo (Italian)	Very loud	
pp	Pianissimo (Italian)	Very soft	
	Key signature of A major	Tells you that all F's, C's, and G's are played as F#'s, C#'s, and G#'s	
Allegretto	Allegretto (Italian)	Lively, quick tempo, but not as fast as Allegro	

Practice: 1. Clap & count 2. Arco

Faster and Louder (Duet) Look for a new dynamic marking.

Boothbay Reel

Minuet Look for another new dynamic marking.

Franklin deLong (unknown–1776)

Sixteenth Shuffle

Tonawanda Polka

Skip to My Lou

Traditional American Folk Song

Sing: Skip, skip, skip to my Lou, Skip, skip, skip to my Lou, Skip to my Lou, my dar-lin'.

sempre f

Fly's in the but-ter-milk, shoo, fly, shoo, Fly's in the but-ter-milk, shoo, fly, shoo, Skip to my Lou, my dar-lin'.

sempre p

Finger Tips

C♯ on the G String, G♯ on the D, E, and G Strings, A Major Scale

When playing C♯ on the G string, be sure to keep all fingers curved, and pull your elbow around and under the violin.

A Major Scale

Exploring C♯

A sharp or flat that is not in the key signature is called an *accidental*.

35

Exploring G♯

36

Waltzing A-Round Play as a round.

37

Another G♯ (Violins and Basses)

38

G♯ on the G String Extend your first finger back to play this G♯.

39

Exploring the A Major Scale

40

Exploring Arpeggios

41

Exploring Thirds

42

A Finger Mixer

43

Moderato

9

Putting It Together

Sea **Chantey**

Traditional English Folk Song

The Hopeful Lover

Traditional Scottish Fiddle Tune

Mockingbird

A. Hawthorne

Lumberman's Song

Be careful to notice the accidentals!

Finnish Folk Song

Rondo

Jacques-Féréol Mazas (1782–1849)

ARCO'S HISTORY HIGHLIGHTS

In 1816, a German named Johann Maelzel invented the *metronome,* a clock-like machine that produced a ticking sound to help musicians keep a steady beat. Ludwig van Beethoven was the first composer to use metronome settings to indicate the tempo of his music (for example, M.M. =112). Metronomes now come in many modern varieties, and they are very helpful for developing a strong sense of rhythm. Try playing the exercises in Unit 2 using a metronome.

Trepak (Duet)

This **trepak** is a famous dance movement
from Tchaikovsky's **ballet** the *Nutcracker*.

Allegro (♩= 112)

Peter Ilyich Tchaikovsky (1840–1893)

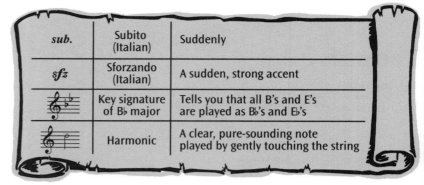

UNIT 3

Ready, Set, Bow

More Eighth Rests, Moving Sixteenth Notes, Sforzando

sub.	Subito (Italian)	Suddenly
sfz	Sforzando (Italian)	A sudden, strong accent
Key signature of B♭ major		Tells you that all B's and E's are played as B♭'s and E♭'s
Harmonic		A clear, pure-sounding note played by gently touching the string

Exploring Eighth Rests (Duet) Practice: 1. Clap & count 2. Sing using solfège 3. Arco

50

Sing: Do Sol Mi…

Further Explorations

51

Bizzy Waltz Look out for sudden dynamic changes!

52

HOT SHOT CHALLENGE
Try playing line 52 once again, this time alternating subito ff and subito pp every other measure.

Theme from Rosamunde

Franz Schubert (1797–1828)

53

Moving Sixteenths

54

George Frideric Handel (1685–1759)

Bourrée

55

Finger Tips

E♭ on the D and A Strings,
B♭ on the E String,
B♭ Major Scale, Harmonics

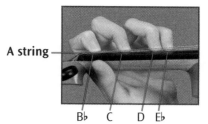

A string — B♭ C D E♭

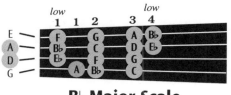

B♭ Major Scale

Exploring E♭ To play E♭ on the D string, reach back with your first finger. Be careful not to move your thumb.

56

Another E♭ (Violins and Violas) To play E♭ on the A string, place your fourth finger "low," directly next to your third finger.

57

One More E♭ (Violas and Cellos)

58

A New B♭ for Violins To play B♭ on the E string, place your fourth finger "low," directly next to your third finger.

59

Exploring the B♭ Major Scale

60

Exploring Arpeggios

61

Exploring Thirds

62

Exploring Harmonics

Harmonics are played by lightly touching the string with a finger. To play harmonics in the following exercises, move your left hand and thumb up the fingerboard as a unit while swinging your left elbow under the instrument, and gently touch the note with your fourth finger.

a. Slide your third finger up the D string as far as you can, as in "Wire Gliders" on page 3.

b. Slide your fourth finger up the D string as far as you can.

c. Play A with your fourth finger on the D string, then lighten your finger and gently touch the string as you slide up, stopping on the D harmonic, one octave above open D (marked ⁴/₀), halfway between the bridge and nut.

d. Slide up the D string with a light finger to the D harmonic without first playing A.

e. While playing open D, silently move your hand up the fingerboard, then lightly touch the D harmonic with your fourth finger.

f., g., h.   Following the same procedure as for the D string, play harmonics on the G, A, and E strings.

63   a.   b.   c.   d.   e.   f.   g.   h.

Putting It Together

Brandenburg Concerto No. 2 Be careful to contrast staccato and tenuto bowings.

Johann Sebastian Bach (1685–1750)

Rondeau

Jean-Joseph Mouret (1682–1738)

Waltz

Johannes Brahms (1833–1897)

Overture to the Barber of Seville Be sure to "retake" another up bow after each lift.

Gioacchino Rossini (1792–1868)

Hunters' Chorus from Der Freischütz (Duet)

This chorus is from Weber's famous opera *Der Freischütz.*

Carl Maria von Weber (1786–1826)

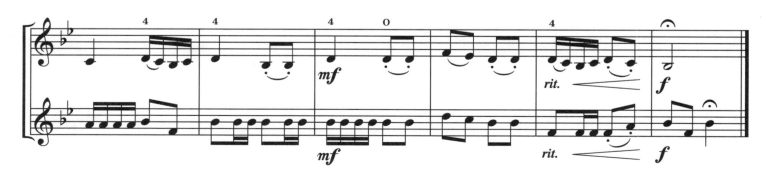

Themes from
Violin Concerto

Antonio Vivaldi (1678–1741)
Arr. R. Meyer

Melody

16

A *concerto* is a large composition for a soloist (or group of soloists), with accompaniment that is usually played by an orchestra. The single solo part contrasts with the accompaniment part. Composers began writing pieces using the concerto form during the Baroque period, and have been doing so ever since. Antonio Vivaldi, a great Italian Baroque composer, wrote this violin concerto, which is frequently played by young students. Be sure to play it with great energy and attention to dynamic changes.

Themes from
Violin Concerto

Accompaniment

Antonio Vivaldi (1678–1741)
Arr. R. Meyer

Exploring Music Theory

We have already learned the solfège syllables for the key of D:

When using a different key signature, we use *movable Do* to change the syllables so that Do becomes the syllable of the first note of the new scale, Re is the second note, and so on:

Write the solfège syllables under the notes of the following melody in G major, then sing and play the line.

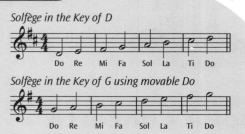

Solfège in the Key of D

Do Re Mi Fa Sol La Ti Do

Solfège in the Key of G using movable Do

Do Re Mi Fa Sol La Ti Do

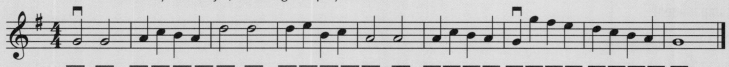

Exploring Ear Training   1. Sing   2. Play   3. Play starting on the note C (transposing)   4. Play starting on other notes

America

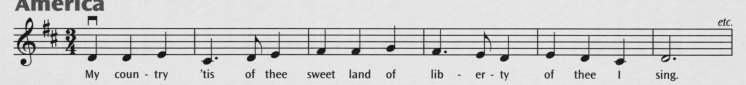

My coun-try 'tis of thee sweet land of lib-er-ty of thee I sing.

Exploring Composition

In the key of G major, the chord made up by the notes G, B, and D is called the *tonic*. The tonic chord is also named using the Roman numeral I. The bugle call "Taps," below, uses only the notes of this chord.

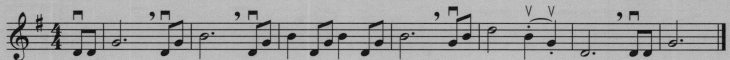

Using only the notes of the tonic chord in G major, compose your own four-measure bugle call with eighth, quarter and half notes. For what might it be used? Give your bugle call a title, then play it.

_____
(title)

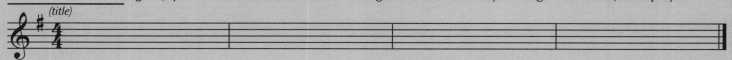

Exploring Improvisation

Choose one note from the A blues scale, and improvise your own one-note melody using the rhythms below. Play along with "Rockin' Rosalyn Blues" on the accompaniment CD, track no. 138.

The A Blues Scale

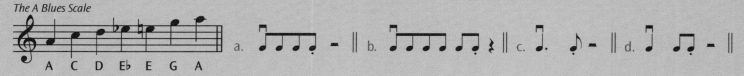

A C D E♭ E G A

Exploring World Music

As a nation of immigrants, Australia has many folk fiddling tunes with roots in other nations. Tunes with British and Celtic origins are very common, as they are in the United States. "Mudgee Waltz" has been called the best-known Australian waltz, and reflects this heritage.

Mudgee Waltz

Australian Fiddle Tune

Ready, Set, Bow

Dotted Eighth+Sixteenth Note, Notes with Slashes, Tremolo

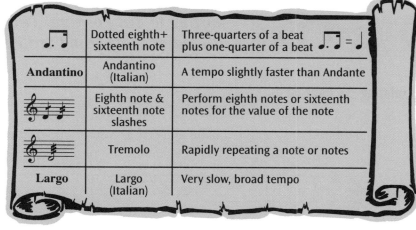

♪. ♪	Dotted eighth+ sixteenth note	Three-quarters of a beat plus one-quarter of a beat ♪.♪ = ♩
Andantino	Andantino (Italian)	A tempo slightly faster than Andante
(slashes)	Eighth note & sixteenth note slashes	Perform eighth notes or sixteenth notes for the value of the note
(tremolo)	Tremolo	Rapidly repeating a note or notes
Largo	Largo (Italian)	Very slow, broad tempo

Exploring Dotted Eighth Notes (Duet)

Practice: 1. Clap & count 2. Arco

69

Clementine   First sing "Clementine" using solfège and movable Do.

Traditional American Folk Song

70

Sing: Do Do Do Sol Mi Mi Mi Do Do Mi…

Slashes   Play notes with a single slash as separate eighth notes.

71

Double Slashes   Play the double-slashed notes as separate sixteenth notes.

72

Tremolo City   Using just a few inches of bow, play tremolo by alternating down bow and up bow strokes as rapidly as possible.

73

Arco versus the Zombies   Be sure to use correct bowings. Be careful to hook the dotted eighth+sixteenths in the first two measures.

74

Finger Tips

Shifting to 3rd Position, Two-Octave G Major Scale Using 3rd Position

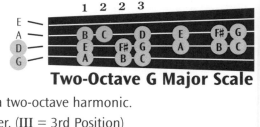

Two-Octave G Major Scale

Exploring 3rd Position (pictures A, B, C)

a. At the "diamond note" G, lift your finger slightly and gently touch the string to play a two-octave harmonic.

b. During the rest, shift your left hand and replace your third finger with your first finger. (III = 3rd Position)

75

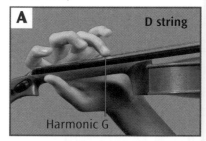

Sliding Up (pictures A, B, C)

a. Shift your first finger from 1st-position E to 3rd-position G, being sure to move your thumb with your first finger. Check the G with the open string.

b. Shift the first finger more quickly into 3rd position, always sliding with the thumb.

76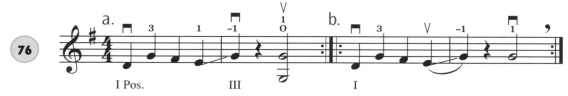

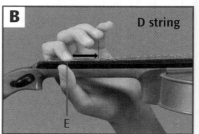

Exploring 3rd-Position Octaves (pictures A, B, C)

a. Shift from 1st to 3rd position with your first finger, always sliding along with the thumb. To shift from 3rd to 1st position, first reach back with your thumb during the rest and draw your hand back to 1st position.

b. Play in tune with the open G drone. Silently slide your first finger and thumb to 3rd position during the rest.

77

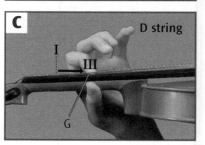

Up the Ladder (pictures C, D)

a. Before beginning the exercise, silently finger E–F#–G, then silently slide your first finger and thumb to 3rd position.

b., c. Staying in 3rd position, play C on the D string with your fourth finger, and play high D on the A string with your first finger. Continue adding fingers on the A string to play more notes.

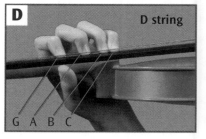

78

Climbing Higher (pictures C, D) Silently finger E–F#–G and shift to 3rd position. Then, play the exercise using only 3rd position.

79

The Two-Octave G Major Scale

Shift quickly to 3rd position after the first F#. Continue to play the second octave in 3rd position.
Remember to lead with the thumb during the rest when shifting back to 1st position.

80

20

Putting It Together

Chester

"Chester" is sometimes referred to as the first national anthem of the United States.

William Billings (1746–1800)

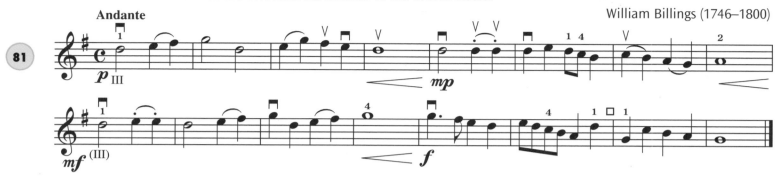

Planxty Irwin

Planxty is an old Irish term meaning "tune" or "song." This planxty probably honors someone with the last name of Irwin.

Turlough O'Carolan (1670–1738)

HOT SHOT CHALLENGE
Play line 82 again,
slurring one bow per measure.

Say Goodbye

Be sure to hook the dotted eighth+sixteenth notes.

Wolfgang Amadeus Mozart (1756–1791)

Alouette

Sing and play "Alouette" with a friend, alternating solo and `tutti` parts.

French-Canadian Folk Song

Sing: Alouette, gentille Alouette. Alouette, je te plumerai.
Je te plumerai la tête, Je te plumerai la tête. Et la tête, et la tête. Alouette, Alouette. Ah!
Alouette, gentille Alouette. Alouette, je te plumerai.

21

ARCO'S HISTORY HIGHLIGHTS

Some of the most marvelous melodies ever written were composed for *operas,* dramatic works in which the dialogue is sung. Orchestras usually accompany the opera singers and also often play long sections of music without any singers. Handel, Mozart, Rossini, Puccini, and Verdi are composers famous for writing great operas.

March from Scipio (Duet)

Handel included this march in his great opera *Scipio.*

George Frideric Handel (1685–1759)

Unit 5

Ready, Set, Bow

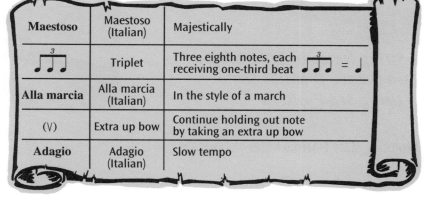

Maestoso	Maestoso (Italian)	Majestically
	Triplet	Three eighth notes, each receiving one-third beat
Alla marcia	Alla marcia (Italian)	In the style of a march
(V)	Extra up bow	Continue holding out note by taking an extra up bow
Adagio	Adagio (Italian)	Slow tempo

Triplets

Exploring Triplets   Practice: 1. Clap & count   2. Arco
Be sure to play the triplets evenly without rushing.

86

Twins and Triplets

87

Waltzing Around   Play as a round. Take an extra up bow on the last note.

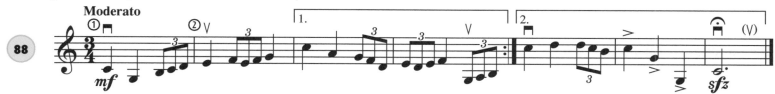

88

Variation on a Familiar Tune   Compose new words to this variation on "This Old Man." Can you sing the tune using solfège? (Hint: the first notes are Sol Mi Mi Mi Sol.)

89

Jiggy

90

March of the Explorers

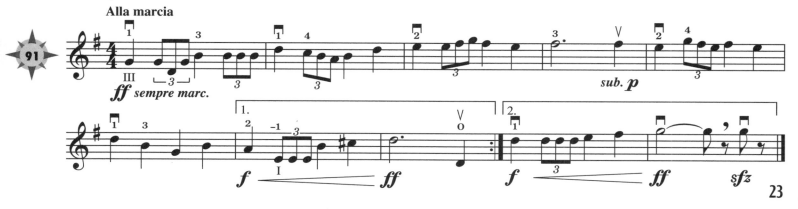

91

23

Finger Tips

E-String Notes in 3rd Position,
Two-Octave D Major Scale
Using 3rd Position

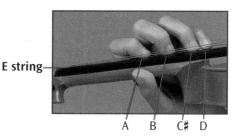

E string

A B C# D

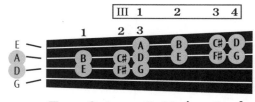

Two-Octave D Major Scale

Exploring More E-String Notes (Violas) This exercise includes A, B, C#, and D on the E-string in 3rd position.

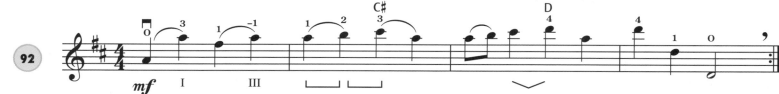

Exploring F# on the C String (Violas and Cellos)

Exploring Another C# (Violas and Cellos)

The Two-Octave D Major Scale

Exploring Arpeggios

Exploring Thirds

HOT SHOT CHALLENGE
After learning lines 95, 96, and 97 as written, try memorizing them. Then play all three lines using the bowings and rhythms at the bottom of page 5.

March in D

Play the entire march in 3rd position.
Write fingerings on the lines provided.

Johann Sebastian Bach
(1685–1750)

Putting It Together

March of the Nutcracker

Peter Ilyich Tchaikovsky (1840–1893)

ARCO'S HISTORY HIGHLIGHTS

String players throughout the world enjoy playing the folk songs and dances of their homelands as well as those of other cultures. This unit includes two waltzes, a familiar folk song, a jig, and an air—all different forms of folk music. Composers of classical music often borrow the special rhythms and melodies of folk music to use in their pieces.

EXPLORING FOLK MUSIC: Look back at the music you have already learned and see how many examples of folk music you can find.

A Scottish Air
Play this air legato, at the correct tempo.

New World Symphony

Antonin Dvořák (1841–1904)

Spanish Fork Waltz

25

Grand March from Aïda (Duet)

The great Italian composer Giuseppe Verdi included this march in his famous opera *Aida*.

Giuseppe Verdi (1813–1901)

26

ARCO DAKOTA'S ACTIVITY PAGE 2

Exploring Music Theory

In the orchestra, the three most commonly used clefs are treble clef 𝄞, alto clef 𝄡, and bass clef 𝄢. With your teacher and friends, discuss which instruments use each clef, and why you think different instruments use different clefs.

Write the following whole notes correctly in each clef.

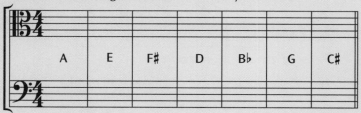

Exploring Ear Training   1. Sing   2. Play in 3rd position starting with first finger on D   3. Write in all the fingerings you used

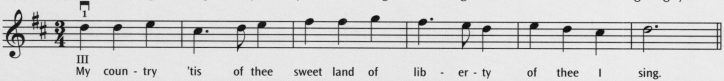

My coun - try 'tis of thee sweet land of lib - er - ty of thee I sing.

Exploring Composition

In the key of G major, the chord built on the fifth note of the scale, D, is called the *dominant*, and consists of the notes D–F#–A. The Roman numeral V is used to refer to the dominant chord. The notes from the I chord and the V chord in G major make up the following melody.

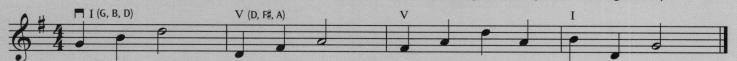

Use the Roman numerals to determine which note is missing from the chord in each measure. Write in each missing note, then play the completed melody.

Exploring Improvisation

Choose three notes from the A blues scale to improvise a melody using the rhythms below. Play along with "Rockin' Rosalyn Blues" on the accompaniment CD, track no. 138.

The A Blues Scale

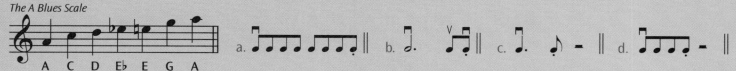

A C D Eb E G A

Exploring World Music

Diddly-Bow Blues

The one-stringed diddly-bow is a traditional African-American instrument, often played by many rural Southern blues singers to accompany themselves. You can pretend you're playing a diddly-bow by holding your violin flat in your lap. With your left hand on top of the violin neck, use only your first finger to slide up and down the A string as you pluck the correct notes with your right thumb. Try singing the words as you accompany yourself.

Moderato

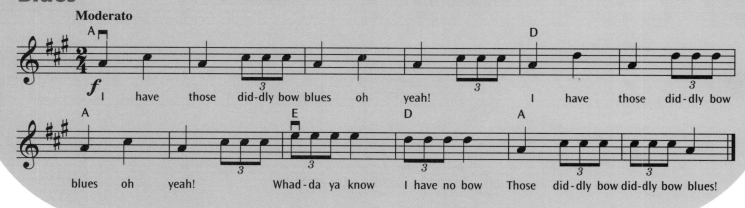

I have those did-dly bow blues oh yeah! I have those did-dly bow

blues oh yeah! Whad-da ya know I have no bow Those did-dly bow did-dly bow blues!

Overture to
La Gazza Ladra
(The Thieving Magpie)

Gioacchino Rossini (1792–1868)
Arr. R. Meyer

Melody

28

Overture to
La Gazza Ladra
(The Thieving Magpie)

An *overture* is an orchestral piece that introduces a variety of themes that will be heard later in a larger composition. For this reason, an overture is usually played at the beginning of a ballet, an opera, or an oratorio. Gioacchino Rossini wrote 40 wonderful operas, each with an overture. The overture to *La Gazza Ladra* is a fine example of how Rossini could weave a variety of contrasting melodies from an opera into one delightful—and challenging—orchestral piece.

Accompaniment

Gioacchino Rossini (1792–1868)
Arr. R. Meyer

Ready, Set, Bow

§ Time Signature, Portato/Louré

§	Time signature	6 = six beats per measure 8 = ♪ or ♪ gets one beat
	Portato (Italian) Louré (French)	Play slurred notes with a slight separation
Marziale	Marziale (Italian)	With a martial (military-like) feel

Exploring § Practice: 1. Clap & count 2. Arco

Here are two ways to count § meter: In a slow tempo, count *in 6;* in a fast tempo, count *in 2.*

105

In 6: 1 2 3 4 5 6   1 2 3 4 5 6
In 2: 1 + a 2 + a   1 + a 2 + a

Further Explorations in § Practice: 1. Clap & count 2. Arco

106

In 6: 1 2 3 4 5 6   1 2 3 4 5 6
In 2: 1 + a 2 + a   1 + a 2 + a

Exploring Rests in § Practice: 1. Clap & count (be sure to speak or count the rests) 2. Arco

107

In 6: 1 2 3 4 5 6   1 2 3 4 5 6   1 2 3 4 5 6
In 2: 1 + a 2 + a   1 + a 2 + a   1 + a 2 + a

Rosalyn's Portato Boat

Play as a round. A slur with a line means to slightly separate the notes by gently stopping the bow.
This bowing is called *portato* (Italian) or *louré* (French).

108

ARCO'S HISTORY HIGHLIGHTS

Ludwig van Beethoven wrote nine magnificent symphonies. His sixth symphony is famous for the way its melodies paint a musical picture of a thunderstorm and the peaceful calm after the storm. Because it is a symphony about nature, it has become known as the *Pastoral Symphony.* What exactly does *pastoral* mean? How can you play this next duet to make it sound pastoral?

Theme from the Pastoral Symphony (Duet) Try singing solfège on line b.

Ludwig van Beethoven (1770–1827)

109

a.

b.

Sing: Do Mi Sol Do…

Finger Tips

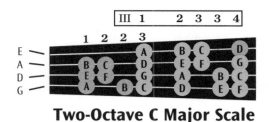
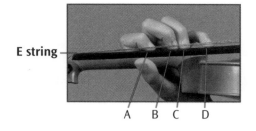

Two-Octave C Major Scale

Shifting on the G String, Two-Octave C Major Scale Using 3rd Position

Exploring Shifting in C Major

Let your left elbow come around under the violin to help you shift on the G string.
Remember to always let your first finger be the "guide finger" as you shift.

110

Shifting Away

111

The Two-Octave C Major Scale

Be careful to shift a whole step in measure 2, and also notice the new finger pattern in 3rd position on the A string.

112

The C Major Scale in a New Rhythm (Violins in 3rd Position)

Silently shift to 3rd position before beginning this scale.

113

Exploring Arpeggios

114

Exploring Thirds

A new shift! In measure 5, slide back to 1st position on your *second* finger. Remember to move your thumb back first.

115

Over the C Swing the eighth notes!

116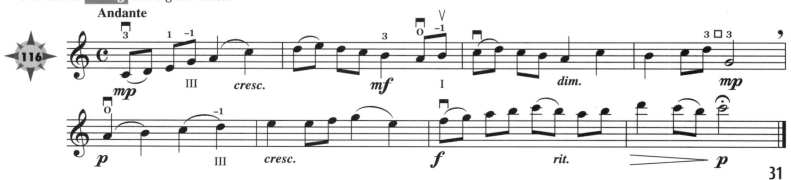

31

Putting It Together

Krishna

Be sure to make a difference between the way you play the slurred notes and portato notes.

Folk Song of India

Irish Washerwoman (Duet)

This is a famous Irish jig in 6/8 time.

Traditional Irish Fiddle Tune

HOT SHOT CHALLENGE

Try playing in true Irish fiddle style by adding some ornaments to the "Irish Washerwoman." Choose from the examples below and see if you can play them throughout the tune. Use your imagination!

The Moldau

Melody

Bedřich Smetana (1824–1884)
Arr. R. Meyer

The Moldau

Many composers of the Romantic era enjoyed writing a form of music known as the *tone poem*. Tone poems are compositions that musically represent a story or specific impressions of the composer. Bedrich Smetana, a Czech composer, wrote a tone poem titled *Ma Vlast (My Country)* in which he musically describes his homeland. One section of this piece, "The Moldau," is named for a great river that flows through the Czech countryside. Listen carefully to how Smetana uses flowing rhythms and melodies to create a musical picture of the magnificent, surging, rushing river.

Accompaniment

Bedřich Smetana (1824–1884)
Arr. R. Meyer

Exploring Music Theory

Enharmonics are two notes that sound the same but have different names. To find another name for a sharp note, find the letter name of the next higher note and add a flat. For example, to find the enharmonic name for F♯, go to the next higher note name, G, and add a flat sign to get G♭: F♯=G♭. To find another name for a flat note, go down to the next note name and add a sharp.

Using the rules above, write the enharmonic for each of the following notes:

C♯ = ___ B♭= ___ G♯= ___ E♭= ___ G♭= ___ A♯= ___ D♯= ___ A♭= ___ D♭= ___

Discuss the following four exceptions to these rules with your teacher: E♯=F, F♭=E, B♯=C, C♭=B.

Exploring Ear Training

Play using only your left-hand first finger, starting in 3rd position.

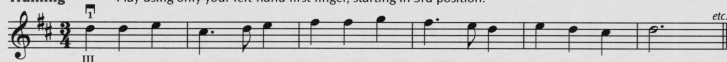

Exploring Composition

In the key of G major, the chord built on the fourth note of the scale, C, is called the *subdominant*. It consists of the notes C–E–G. The Roman numeral **IV** is used to refer to the subdominant chord. The following melody uses the three chords we have learned: the tonic, dominant, and subdominant. Name each chord by writing **I**, **V**, or **IV** in the box above each measure.

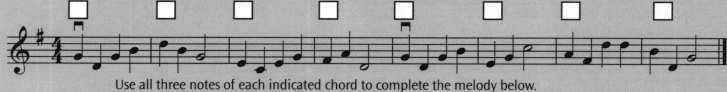

Use all three notes of each indicated chord to complete the melody below.
Then, label the chords used in measures 1, 2, 4, and 6. Play the melody.

Exploring Improvisation

Choose four notes from the A blues scale to improvise a melody using the 2-bar rhythms below. Play along with "Rockin' Rosalyn Blues" on the accompaniment CD, track no. 138.

The A Blues Scale

A   C   D   E♭   E   G   A

Exploring World Music

When the Spanish settled Mexico in what is now the Southwest United States, they brought with them their musical traditions. Over time, these traditions—which included $\frac{6}{8}$ rhythms, the use of violins, trumpets, and many kinds of guitars—developed into Mexican mariachi music. Today, this music usually includes all of these instruments, and has become extremely popular on both sides of the Mexico/U.S. border. Notice that $\frac{6}{8}$ time usually feels "in two," but sometimes is felt "in three."

Mariachi Son

Allegro

UNIT 7

Ready, Set, Bow

Cut Time, Spiccato

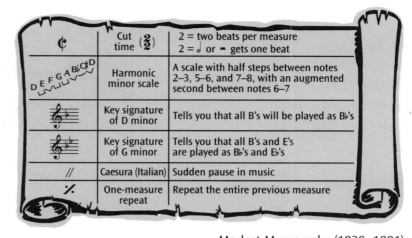

¢	Cut time ($\frac{2}{2}$)	2 = two beats per measure 2 = ♩ or ⁀ gets one beat
D E F G A B♭ C♯ D	Harmonic minor scale	A scale with half steps between notes 2–3, 5–6, and 7–8, with an augmented second between notes 6–7
(treble clef)	Key signature of D minor	Tells you that all B's will be played as B♭'s
(treble clef)	Key signature of G minor	Tells you that all B's and E's are played as B♭'s and E♭'s
//	Caesura (Italian)	Sudden pause in music
✗.	One-measure repeat	Repeat the entire previous measure

Great Gate of Kiev Sustain the notes for their full value. Feel the rhythm in two broad beats.

Modest Mussorgsky (1839–1881)

122
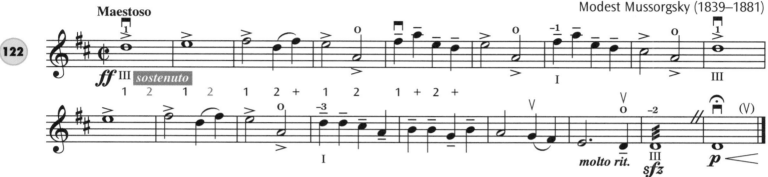

British Grenadiers Practice: 1. Clap & count 2. Sing using solfège 3. Arco

Traditional British March

123

Exploring Spiccato

Spiccatto is a short, bouncing bow stroke. To prepare spiccato, grip the string by adding weight in the bow (A). Release the weight so the bow pops out of the string and is allowed to bounce on the notes that follow (B). Be sure the bow moves mostly right to left while bouncing slightly off the string.

124
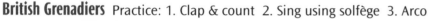

Farandole (Duet) Keep the spiccato notes very steady. Try practicing with a metronome.

Georges Bizet (1838–1875)

125

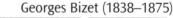

37

Finger Tips

Augmented Second,
D Harmonic Minor,
G Harmonic Minor

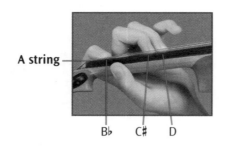

A string

B♭ C♯ D

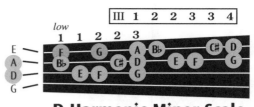

D Harmonic Minor Scale

A New Interval The interval between B♭ and C♯ is called an augmented second (⁓).

126

mf

D Major Scale Mark all the half steps with a ∨ sign.

127

mf

The D Harmonic Minor Scale D minor is called the *parallel minor* to D major. Be sure to exaggerate the low B♭ and the high C♯.

128

mf

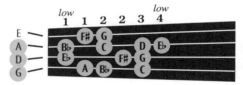

G Harmonic Minor Scale

Minor Mixer Mark all the augmented seconds with a ⁓ sign.

129

mf

G Major Scale Mark all the half steps with a ∨ sign.

130

mf

The G Harmonic Minor Scale G minor is called the *parallel minor* to G major. Be sure to exaggerate the low E♭ and the high F♯.

131

mf

HOT SHOT CHALLENGE
Try playing thirds using the
D harmonic minor scale, then
the G harmonic minor scale.

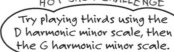

Putting It Together

Theme from Symphony No. 1

Play as a round. This is a minor variation on a familiar theme. Can you tell which one?

Gustav Mahler (1860–1911)

Partita

Johann Sebastian Bach (1685–1750)

Hatikvah This famous Hebrew melody is in the key of _____ _____ .
(write your answer)

National Anthem of Israel

Inspector Guy Swing the eighth notes.

The Wild Horseman Be sure to play all the eighth notes spiccato.

Robert Schumann (1810–1856)

ARCO'S HISTORY HIGHLIGHTS

In the course of his tragically short life, Wolfgang Amadeus Mozart composed an astounding amount of music for string instruments, including 5 violin concertos, 37 violin sonatas, nearly two dozen string quartets, and 41 symphonies. The following theme is from the first `movement` of Mozart's *Symphony No. 40,* which is one of his most well known works.

Theme from Symphony No. 40 (Duet)

To play this famous theme by Mozart, contrast line a's legato slurs with the spiccato bowing of line b. Don't rush, and keep the eighth notes steady.

Wolfgang Amadeus Mozart (1756–1791)

Exploring Music Theory

Rewrite this melody in cut time, then write the solfège syllables below the notes. Be sure to notice the key signature! Sing and play the melody—it should sound the same as the original.

Exploring Ear Training

Change the key signature to one flat and play "America" in the key of D minor. Don't forget the C sharps.

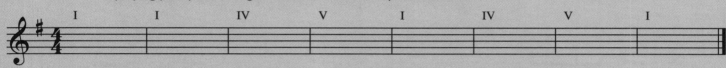

etc.

Exploring Composition

Use eighth, quarter and half notes to compose your own melody in G major. Follow the *chord progression* (order of chords) shown above the staff, using only notes from the chord given in each measure. Play your composition, then try playing your piece along with another student's piece as a duet.

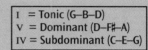

I = Tonic (G–B–D)
V = Dominant (D–F♯–A)
IV = Subdominant (C–E–G)

Exploring Improvisation

Choose any notes from the A blues scale and improvise your own melody using the 4-bar rhythms below. Play along with "Rockin' Rosalyn Blues" on the accompaniment CD, track no. 138.

The A Blues Scale

A   C   D   E♭   E   G   A

Exploring World Music

Fiddling has long been an important folk tradition in Sweden. In each village, the fiddler (or *spielman*) enjoys a significant role, performing music for important community events such as dances, festivals, and even government ceremonies. Wedding marches such as this one are commonly provided by a fiddler or a group of fiddlers playing in harmony.

Wedding March from Jamtland

Swedish Fiddle Tune

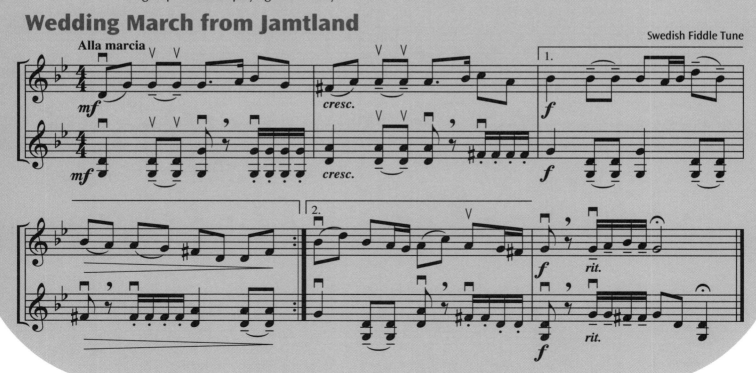

A Night at the Ballet

Melody

Arr. R. Meyer

Musical compositions written especially for ballet are some of the most delightful pieces a string player can perform! When writing  music, composers try to include expressive rhythms and melodies that will help the dancers tell stories through their movements. This piece includes a variety of themes from many ballets of different music periods. It begins with a polka from the ballet *Sylvia* by Leo Delibes, which is followed by a theme from Tchaikovsky's famous ballet *Swan Lake.* "Simple Gifts," the American Shaker melody used by Aaron Copland in his music for the ballet *Appalachian Spring,* is next. The "Russian Sailors' Dance" from Gliere's *The Red Poppy* is played just before another famous Tchaikovsky melody, the "Sleeping Beauty Waltz," is heard. The piece closes with a stirring melody from Igor Stravinsky's 20th-century ballet *The Firebird.* Imagine how dancers might respond with movement to each of these different melodies.

A Night at the Ballet

Accompaniment

Arr. R. Meyer

Bill Cheatham
from *Fiddlers Philharmonic Encore*

"Bill Cheatham" is a lively reel that has become common in the bluegrass fiddle repertoire. The basic version, played quickly, is quite an energetic melody; but when syncopated rhythms, uneven bowings and flatted *blue notes* are added, the tune takes on the hard-driving feel that has made bluegrass so popular all over the world. The first two sections (mm. 3–18) make up the basic melody. The third and fourth sections (mm. 19–34) are a variation, sometimes called a *break,* or solo. Using some of the musical ideas and the chord symbols in the break section, try to create an improvisation of your own.

EXPLORING THE BLUES

138 # Rockin' Rosalyn Blues

One of the most important musical forms to develop in America is the blues, originating from the old work songs and "field hollers" of African-American slaves in the South. The blues often includes repeated musical ideas called *riffs*, and also features improvisation. "Rockin' Rosalyn Blues" is in a form called the *12-bar blues* and is based upon a well-known progression of chords. The Solo or Tune should be played with the Background.

1. Take turns playing either the Tune or the Solo with the Background part.

2. Using the skills learned in the "Exploring Improvisation" sections of the Activity Pages, try to improvise your own version of the Tune.

3. Create your own arrangement. Decide who should play each part, and the order in which to play the Tune, Solo, and Improvisation.

EXPLORING SCALES

C Major Scale

G Major Scale

G Minor Scale

D Major Scale

D Minor Scale

A Major Scale

F Major Scale

B♭ Major Scale

Glossary

adagio (*It.*) Slow tempo 23

air A song, melody or tune 25

alla marcia (*It.*) In the style of a march. 23

allegro (*It.*) Fast, lively, quick or cheerful tempo 6

allegretto (*It.*) Lively, quick tempo, slightly slower than *allegro*. 8

andante (*It.*) Moving, moderate *tempo*; "walking" speed 6

andantino (*It.*) A tempo slightly faster than *andante* 19

arpeggio (*It.*) A chord played one note after another 5

a tempo (*It.*) Return to the original tempo 7

augmented Raised 38

ballet A drama presented by dancers with musical accompaniment 11

bourrée (*Fr.*) A 17th-century French dance in quick $\frac{2}{4}$ or $\frac{4}{4}$ time. 12

cantabile (*It.*) In a singing style 14

cesura (///) (*It.*) Indicates a sudden pause in the music. . . . 37

chamber music Music for a small ensemble with each part played by one performer 15

chantey A work song sung by sailors 10

concerto (*It*). A composition for soloist(s) accompanied by orchestra 6

cut time (¢) Indicates the half note gets one beat instead of the quarter note (sometimes seen as $\frac{2}{2}$) 37

détaché (*Fr.*) Detached; one bow per note 4

divisi (*div.*) (*It.*) Divide parts; indicates that two parts written on one staff are to be played by different performers 39

fortissimo (*ff*) (*It.*) Very loud 8

harmonic A clear, pure-sounding note played by gently touching the string 12

harmonic minor A scale with half steps between notes 2–3, 5–6, and 7–8, with an augmented second between notes 6–7 37

hook (♪♪) Indicates that two or more notes should be played in the same bow direction, stopping the bow between notes 4

improvisation The process of creating music spontaneously. . 18

interval The distance, or number of musical steps, between notes 38

jig A popular 16th-century dance in $\frac{6}{8}$ time 25

largo (*It.*) Very slow, broad tempo 19

legato (*It.*) Played smoothly 25

leggiero (*It.*) Played lightly, delicately 8

louré (♪♪♪) (*Fr.*) Bowing in which slurred notes are played with a slight separation (see *portato*) . . 30

maestoso (*It.*) Majestically 23

marcato (*marc.*) (*It.*) Marked, stressed, separate bow strokes 4

marziale (*It.*) Played with a martial (military-like) feeling 30

minuet An old, French dance in $\frac{3}{4}$ time 8

M.M. Abbreviation for "Maelzel's metronome;" used for metronome settings to indicate how many times the metronome will tick per minute (for example, M.M.=112) 10

moderato (*It.*) Moderate tempo 6

molto (*It.*) Much or very 14

movement An independent section of a larger musical work such as a symphony 40

nocturne A Romantic piece in a melancholy mood 7

opera A dramatic work in which the text is sung 15

overture An orchestral piece that introduces themes in a ballet, opera, or oratorio 14

partita A composition with a number of short movements. 39

pianissimo (*pp*) (*It.*) Very soft 8

polka A fast dance with two beats to a measure that originated in Bohemia in 1830 8

portato (♪♪) (*It.*) Slurred notes played with a slight separation (see *louré*) 30

reel A lively dance, usually in $\frac{4}{4}$ time 8

rondeau, rondo A musical form with a repeating theme that alternates with contrasting themes . . . 14, 10

sempre (*It.*) Always 8

sforzando (*sfz*) (*It.*) A sudden, strong accent 12

shuffle A repetitive rhythmic figure often used in fiddle music, usually consisting of an eighth note followed by two sixteenth notes. 32

solfège Method of singing that uses syllables assigned to the notes of the scale (Do, Re, Mi, Fa, Sol, La, Ti, Do) 5

solo Music played by a single player (soloist) 21

sostenuto (*It.*) Sustained 37

spiccato (*It.*) Play by bouncing the bow on the string . . . 37

subito (*sub.*) (*It.*) Suddenly 12

swing Play eighth notes unevenly, with a lilt 31

symphony A large composition for orchestra, usually having four *movements* 30

syncopation A rhythmic pattern in which the natural accent is shifted to the off-beat 4

tenuto (♩) (*It.*) Played long and connected 4

theme A main tune or melody of a composition. 12

tone poem A composition that musically represents a story or specific impressions of the composer . 35

tremolo (♪) (*It.*) Rapidly repeated note or notes 19

trepak A lively Russian dance in $\frac{2}{4}$ time. 11

triplet (♪♪♪) Three notes played in the same time as two notes of the same value 23

tutti (*It.*) Everyone plays. 21

waltz A dance in $\frac{3}{4}$ time that originated in the late 18th century 25

EXPLORER'S MAP

The noble schooner *Musicianship* has set sail, and YOU are already aboard! This secret nautical chart plots the course you must take across the Sea of Knowledge. The great String Explorers Arco Dakota and Rosalyn Le Bow have sailed these waters before, and will guide you through many passages and past important landmarks. Complete each checkpoint, and soon you will disembark in the Lands of Golden Harmony, with a passport to enter the kingdom through the Notable Gates of Merit!

START

Musicianship

Unit 4
80

Unit 4
85

Unit 5
91

Unit 4
74

Unit 5
95

Unit 1
24

Unit 5
101

Unit 2
33

Unit 6
109

Unit 7
131

Unit 3
64

Unit 3
62

Unit 6
116

Unit 7
128

Unit 7
137

Unit 2
42

Bill
Cheatham

Unit 3
55

Unit 7
125

Unit 2
48

Unit 6
120